BANFF
NATIONAL PARK

Text by
CARL BENN

Photographs by
ANDREA PISTOLESI

D1343752

BONECHI

Distributor:

Canadian Souvenir Sales Ltd.

Golden Eagle Building, Highway 93/95
Tel. (250) 347 9628
Fax: (250) 347 9011
Box 99, Radium Hot Springs
British Columbia
Canada V0A 1M0

ISBN 1-895154-16-5

BANFF NATIONAL PARK

(abstract from the book ''Canadian Rockies'')
Project and editorial conception: Casa Editrice Bonechi
Publication Manager: Monica Bonechi
Picture research: Monica Bonechi
Cover, Graphic design and Make-up: Manuela Ranfagni
Editing: Anna Baldini

Text: Carl Benn
Maps: Stefano Benini

© Copyright by Casa Editrice Bonechi - Florence - Italy
E-mail: bonechi@bonechi.it - Internet: www.bonechi.it

ISBN 88-8029-822-4

New York Address:
98 Thompson Street # 38 - New York, N.Y. 10012
Ph: (212) 343-9235 - Fax: (212) 625-9636
e-mail: bonechinyc@aol.com

Printed in Italy by Centro Stampa Editoriale Bonechi.

Photographs from archives of Casa Editrice Bonechi taken by
Andrea Pistolesi.

Photographs by courtesy of Canadian Souvenir Sales Ltd.:
pages 10 (below), 22 (below),44 (above), 47 (below left), by John Bicknell;
pages 44 (below left and right), 47(below right), by Timothy G.M. Reynolds.

* * *

INTRODUCTION

The magnificent Canadian Rockies are one of the world's most popular tourist destinations - and for good reason: they comprise some of the most glorious wilderness lands on earth, but they also are among the most accessible natural environments on the planet. At the same time, the very best in tourism facilities sit readily at hand to cater to a traveller's every need for comfort. Alternatively, those who feel like roughing it can find challenging opportunities to experience mountain and ice climbing, white water rafting, hiking, skiing, and camping in the wild within a few kilometres of the comforts of civilization.

The Rockies consist of several mountain groupings that run roughly along a northwest-southeast axis: the front ranges which lie beside the Alberta foothills, the eastern main ranges (such as those you will encounter at Lake Louise on the Alberta-British Columbia border), the western main ranges inside BC,

Takakkaw Falls, Canada's second tallest at 380 metres in Yoho National Park.

About 11,500 years ago, when the ice sheets were in retreat, the climate had begun to warm, and hunter-gatherer Palaeo-Indians started to appear at the southern and lower elevations of the Rocky Mountain and neighbouring regions. The environment they encountered below the mountains was a mix of tundra towards the north and lichen woodlands to the south.

They hunted such now-extinct beasts as ancient mammoths, mastodons, camels, horses, and sloths, as well as creatures indigenous to Canada today such as bison, beavers, and caribou. Gradually the more exotic species disappeared and the climate continued to warm to its present-day state.

The people themselves, ever numerous in the inhospitable environment of the Rockies, adapted to changing conditions and developed more complex and regionally-distinct societies

and the western ranges over by Radium Hot Springs on the border with the Rocky Mountain Trench. The story of the Rockies began hundreds of millions of years ago when the region lay under water. The land to the east drained into the sea, dumping sediment which slowly hardened into the distinctive layers of limestone, shale, dolomite, and quartzite that are so visible on the mountains today. Then, about 200 million years ago, the immense continental plate under North America began to move west and crashed into a series of islands, land masses, and other plates. Over the next 35 million years, these sedimentary layers were compressed horizontally. Subsequently, some of them broke under tremendous pressure and shifted up over the underlying layers, piling upwards, and forming mountains. Now, at an age of 120 million years, the Rockies are older than the Himalayas, the Alps, and the American Rockies. They also have been eroded significantly from the time of their primeval birth because the sedimentary rock that composes the mountains is susceptible to the forces of wind, water, and ice that have attacked these giant peaks over the millennia.

During the last of the ice ages, which ended about 11,000 years ago, most of Canada lay under massive sheets of ice. In the lowland areas, such as the Bow River Valley in Banff, glaciers transformed the landscape of the old 'V-shaped' river valleys by carving them deeper and wider so that most Rocky Mountain valleys today are more 'U-shaped' than they were before the glaciers descended upon the region.

over the centuries, as demonstrated by the changes in their tools which archaeologists have discovered in the Rockies and elsewhere in western Canada. The first Europeans to reach the Rocky Mountains encountered three main cultural groups, each comprising a number of different nations: the subarctic peoples to the north; and to the south, the plateau cultural group centred west of the mountains, and the inhabitants of the Great Plains to the east.

Before Europeans came to the Rockies, however, their goods arrived, carried here by aboriginal traders who acquired them from fur trade outposts at Hudson Bay and elsewhere. Similarly, modern horses reached the area in the early 1700s after making their way north from Spanish Mexico. By the 1750s, European explorers began to venture into what now is Alberta. Because of fierce competition between the Hudson's Bay Company of London and its rival, the North West Company in Montreal, fur trade posts began to be built in the province by the 1780s. Many fur trade employees married into aboriginal society and helped create a new, mixed-race cultural group, the Métis. In 1793, fur trader and explorer Alexander Mackenzie staked his claim to fame when he led the first group of Europeans through the Rockies from the plains to the Pacific Ocean. Christian missionaries arrived in Alberta in the early decades of the 19th century. Then, a trickle of ranchers and settlers moved onto the Alberta foothills east of the Rockies after the Canadian government negotiated treaties with the native inhabitants, beginning

in the 1870s. During this period of early exploration and settlement, however, the Rocky Mountains remained relatively quiet.

That changed with the arrival of the railway in the 1880s. Earlier, in 1867, far to the east, the older British colonies of Nova Scotia, New Brunswick, and the United Province of Canada (now Ontario and Quebec) united as the Dominion of Canada, a country within the British Empire. Two years later, the Dominion purchased the vast Hudson's Bay Company territory representing what now forms part of northern Quebec and Ontario, the totality of Manitoba, Saskatchewan, and Alberta, and much of the Yukon and Northwest Territories. Then, in 1871, British Columbia joined the Canadian confederation. However, there was a condition: a transcontinental railway had to be built linking it to the rest of Canada through the Rocky Mountains. In 1883, that railway, the celebrated Canadian Pacific, reached Banff from the east. Work continued for another two years, and in November 1885, the last spike of the transcontinental railway was driven into the ground at Craigellachie in the Eagle Pass of British Columbia. The first train to make the journey from eastern Canada to the Pacific left Montreal in June 1886. Afterwards, large numbers of settlers, miners, and others moved to Alberta and British Columbia and began the process of creating the modern society that now is home to the

Lake Louise, a glorious spot in Banff National Park.

Pretty Peyto Lake on the Icefields Parkway between Banff and Jasper.

several million people who live in Canada's two westernmost provinces.

The advent of the railway allowed for the birth of mining and forestry in the Rockies. With good rail connections, coal mining and logging became major activities at Banff and Jasper in late Victorian times, while talc, iron, lead, silver, zinc, gold, sulphur, and other minerals encouraged miners to set up operations throughout the Rocky Mountains. Tourism also got its birth in the 1880s because of the railways. Now, travel-trade is the central industry in Banff, Jasper, and much of the rest of the Canadian Rocky Mountains.

Today, the region is well positioned to provide you with all the tourist facilities you will ever need while you enjoy the primary attractions of the Rockies, the stunningly grand scenery and one of the world's great wildernesses. The best of the Rockies is preserved in perpetuity in a number of famous and not-so-famous national and provincial parks.

So important are the Canadian Rocky Mountains to the planet that the United Nations declared them to be a world heritage site in 1984.

Now, at this point in our story, we would like to invite you to join us on a journey through the Canadian Rocky Mountains, to peruse the pages below and enjoy our wonderful photographs, as we explore this fascinating part of the world.

Beautiful poppies on the grounds of the Chateau Lake Louise.

Athabasca Falls, one of Jasper National Park's many attractions.

BANFF NATIONAL PARK

Banff, Alberta sits on the Trans-Canada Highway, 130 kilometres west of Calgary. Founded in 1885, it is Canada's oldest national park. Two years earlier, some railway workers improvised a rough ladder out of a tree to explore a cave that the local natives had used for generations to cure bodily complaints. Inside, the three men discovered sulphurous hot springs which, they realized, had commercial value in an age when 'taking the waters' was a fashionable treatment for whatever ailed people. They built a log cabin nearby, and within a year several small enterprises had opened to cater to guests who wanted to test the restorative powers of the springs. However, arguments arose over who owned Banff's resources. The Canadian government, therefore, created Rocky Mountain Park in a 26-square-kilometre area around the springs to keep them in the public domain. Gradually, the park grew to take in the region's most scenic areas, eventually reaching the

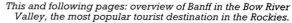

6641 square kilometres encompassed by today's Banff National Park.

The most visible industry in Banff today is tourism. Back in 1888, the general manager of the Canadian Pacific Railway, William Cornelius Van Horne, helped foster that industry when he opened the magnificent Banff Springs Hotel. In Van Horne's view, tourists not only would spend their money eating and sleeping in his hotel, but would take his trains across the country to get here, and thereby rescue the near-bankrupt CPR, and even help the railway prosper. He knew that Banff had the key ingredients to attract affluent Victorian tourists: beautiful scenery, curative hot springs, and the opportunity to indulge in the era's increasingly-popular avocation, 'alpinism,' in which people sought out spectacular mountain environments to increase their knowledge of exotic landscapes and to find transcendence amidst nature's cold and sublimely hostile peaks.

The Banff town site with the baronial Banff Springs Hotel in the background.

This and following pages: overview of Banff in the Bow River Valley, the most popular tourist destination in the Rockies.

BANFF AVENUE

The heart of Banff National Park today is the town of Banff, a community of 7000. Each year four million guests drop in to visit. If you come during the peak winter or summer seasons, you might be forgiven for thinking that every one of them is in town at the same moment as you are while you wait impatiently at the end of a long queue to get a seat in a restaurant or buy an ice cream cone! (A hint: late spring and early autumn are less crowded.) The name of the town and park was a conceit to the two largest shareholders of the Canadian Pacific Railway in the 19th century, Donald Smith and George Stephen, both of whom hailed from Banffshire (now Grampian) in Scotland.

The town's main street is Banff Avenue with its dozens of gift and souvenir shops, restaurants, clubs, and services. Many of the shops sell upscale merchandise, and there are several commercial galleries specializing in native and western art. One of the stores is the Hudson's Bay Company outlet. The HBC had its origins in a royal charter from King Charles II in 1670 to trade furs in and out of Hudson Bay. While the history of the HBC was once the stuff of legend, 'the Bay' now survives primarily as a department store chain. Yet memories of its glory days can be found in its shop where you can purchase such historic items as the famous 'point blankets' of fur trade renown.

CASCADE GARDENS

The administrative centre for Banff is situated in the charming Cascade Gardens at the foot of Banff Avenue. Here, you can enjoy a shaded and flower-filled respite from the bustle of the town, catch your breath, and get the travel information you need to enjoy your Rocky Mountain vacation. Alternatively, you can look back up Banff Avenue towards Cascade Mountain and snap one of the most popular pictures in the Rockies. Developed in the 1930s as a make-work project during the Great Depression, the gardens are just one of a number of interesting attractions in the town. Another is the Buffalo Paddock near the Trans-Canada Highway. There are two kinds of bison (or buffalo) in North America, the wood bison native to this part of the country, and the more famous plains bison. Sadly, the last of the wood bison in the Rockies was killed in 1858 near Lake Louise. The bison you see today are descended from ones shipped in from Wood Buffalo National Park far to the northeast. Rainy-day visitors can fill a few hours at one of Banff's museums: the Park Museum, the Natural History Museum, the Whyte Museum of the Canadian Rockies, and the Luxton Museum which surveys the region's aboriginal story. Culture vultures will enjoy the Banff Centre which offers artistic exhibits, dramatic performances, and music festivals.

Banff Avenue in summer and winter, with Cascade Mountain in the background. Below: gorgeous floral colour abounds at the Cascade Gardens.

BANFF SPRINGS HOTEL

The most prominent human landmark in the Rockies is the Banff Springs Hotel. When new in 1888, it was the world's largest hotel at 250 rooms. Back then, a day's stay cost $3.50. Designed by architect Bruce Price, the Banff Springs was the first of a number of chateau-like hotels the Canadian Pacific Railway would build across Canada. During its first season, it hosted upwards of 5000 guests. That number steadily rose, reaching 10,000 in 1904.

Gradually, the CPR replaced the original building with a new one constructed in the Scottish baronial tradition between 1910 and 1928. As might be expected, the Banff Springs was the address of choice in the Rockies. Therefore, it played host to all sorts of famous people, including heads of state, royalty, and those royals of popular culture, movie stars. Recently renovated by Canadian Pacific Hotels, the Banff Springs can lodge 1700 guests in its 825 rooms who are pampered with superlative services, a spa, good restaurants, comfortable lounges, interesting shops, an Olympic-sized pool, tennis courts, stables, and skating facilities. Even if you're not a guest, don't be shy about visiting and enjoying the hotel grounds and public areas.

The Banff Springs Hotel, a Bow River landmark at the base of Sulphur Mountain since 1888.

Open to the public, the golf course at the Banff Springs Hotel offers one of the world's most scenic rounds of golf. Built with prisoner-of-war labour during World War I, it was redesigned in 1927.

The Bow Falls in the town of Banff near the Banff Springs Hotel. Above: Hoodoos at Tunnel Mountain.

Following pages: the majestic Bow River, just one of the many waterways where you can experience a rafting tour.

BOW RIVER AND FALLS

The town of Banff sits in the Bow Valley between Sulphur and Cascade mountains. The river that cuts through the town is the mighty Bow, which flows 645 kilometres from the glacially-fed waters of Bow Lake, through Banff, and off through Calgary to join the Oldman River. As well as mighty, it's murky too because of glacial till in its waters. In total, it drains an area of 25,300 square kilometres. A popular destination along the river is the Bow Falls, located near the Banff Springs Hotel.

One of the best ways of seeing the Bow River is on a guided, family-oriented rafting trip provided by a commercial operator in the town. This business is just one of hundreds in the Rockies that makes its money from supplying tourists with the services they desire. Thus, the Rockies offer bike and boat rentals, cruises, carriage tours, fishing, golf, horseback riding, kayak and whitewater rafting, and all sorts of outfitting and guided trail tours.

Various forms of accommodation, from primitive campsites to grand hotels, satisfy every taste, and some of Canada's best dining establishments, along with interesting ethnic restaurants, are to be found throughout the region.

HOODOOS

Some of the weirdest rock configurations in the Rockies, visible at such places as Yoho and Banff national parks, are Hoodoos. Typically fashioned from layers of shale and sandstone, these missile-like formations are carved out of the earth by a mix of erosion, wind, rain, and surface water. They range in size from a few humble centimetres to more majestic heights of several metres. Often they are capped with an odd-looking hard rock top which protects the lower parts from deterioration. Once the cap disappears, the hoodoo is doomed to rapid erosion. One legend claims that hoodoos are giants who have been turned to stone, only to awake at night and frighten people by throwing rocks at them. Another asserts that they are teepees inhabited by evil spirits. In the Banff region, you can see four sets of hoodoos with little difficulty. One is located at Tunnel Mountain, another near Canmore, a third at Lake Minnewanka, and a fourth, incomplete set, sits near the Cascade hydro-electric facility. The ones at Lake Minnewanka still have their caps on, while those at Tunnel Mountain are accessible along a short interpretive hiking trail. If you plan to visit other parts of the province, you can find particularly striking hoodoos in the Alberta Badlands.

Inside the cave that gave birth to western Canada's tourism industry. Above: the pool restored to its 1912 appearance.

CAVE AND BASIN CENTENNIAL CENTRE

The cave and basin, discovered in 1883 by three railway workers, are the literal source of the creation of Banff National Park. Back in the late 19th and early 20th centuries, people flocked to the 34-degree-Celsius springs for their supposed curative and restorative powers, and in some cases, just for a hot bath in a world without much plumbing! Shortly after their discovery, the springs offered bath houses and other conveniences where, for 10 cents, people could unwind from the stresses of the Victorian world. In 1888, over 5000 people swam in the waters at the Cave and Basin. Because of intense demand, the government built new facilities beside the cave between 1912 and 1914, including what then was Canada's largest swimming pool.

Sadly, the original cave and basin, along with the pool, gradually became structurally unsound and had to be closed in 1976. With many people disappointed by this unfortunate event, the federal government restored the Cave and Basin, rebuilt the pool to the 1912 design, and recreated an 1886 bath house to add to the historical interest. In 1985, the Cave and Basin Centennial Centre opened to honour the 100th anniversary of the national park system. Now it hosts over a million visitors every year to the historic cave and basin area (open all year).

You can tour the cave and basin and inside these renowned attractions, you will see the original space that the railway workers found in the 1880s, looking much the way it did back then, complete with foul-smelling, sulphurous hot water. You also will see the strange sponge-like calcite rock that dominates the interior, known as tufa, which at some places is seven metres thick. Audio-visual presentations, historical displays, and geological exhibits interpret the story of this curious place. The Cave and Basin complex also boasts a tea room, a terraced picnic area, and the inevitable gift shop. You can enjoy short walks from the centre to explore the cave's immediate surroundings. One visits a nearby marshland to consider how the heated spring water has affected the surrounding ecosystems. Another is a wheelchair-accessible path that takes people to the cave's famous vent opening.

Banff from the gondola; lower: gondola arriving at the summit.
Opposite, upper: Canada's highest restaurant; bottom: the
mountain-top boardwalk.

SULPHUR MOUNTAIN GONDOLA

Sulphur Mountain gets its name from the smell of the hot springs near its base. At 2451 metres, this is a popular peak with visitors since it is easily accessible via gondola. The lift, built in 1959, is one of several in Banff National Park. It whisks you to an elevation of 2285 metres in eight minutes inside roomy, safe, and glass-enclosed gondolas while you gaze out at a sensational 360-degree view of Banff, Cascade Mountain, and the surrounding area. Once at the summit, you can savour the mountain top environment that normally is so hard to reach, while admiring breathtaking views of the Bow River Valley, Lake Minnewanka, and the neighbouring mountains. You can even have dinner at Canada's highest restaurant!

Brown bighorn sheep live on the mountain and may approach you looking for a tasty handout. However, feeding them is not allowed. The largest of these animals weighs about 125 kilograms and stands a metre tall at the shoulders. Typically, they travel in flocks of up to 50 animals under the leadership of a dominant and mature ram, whose position is determined in duels with other rams. While his place in the hierarchy is challenged regularly, the dominant ewe, who decides where the lambs and other ewes will travel during the summer months, often reigns unchallenged for many years.

UPPER HOT SPRINGS AND POOL

The Upper Hot Springs, which have attracted tourists since the 1880s, are situated a short distance from downtown Banff. Fed by the naturally-heated springs of Sulphur Mountain to about 40 degrees Celsius, they provide patrons with a hotter soak than the waters of the more famous Cave and Basin.

Commercial use of these springs began in 1886 when a CPR doctor, R.G. Brett, opened a 'sanitorium,' with water piped from Sulphur Mountain 2400 metres away. Claiming the water could cure almost every complaint, Brett charged what then was a hefty $2.00 a day to use his facilities. At the same time, he built the Grandview Villa right at the Upper Hot Springs themselves where he offered billiards, massages, and non-alcoholic 'temperance' drinks along with his water cures. At one point, canes and crutches were nailed up on the trees at the springs, supposedly by people who no longer needed them after taking the waters. In 1901, Dr Brett's villa at the springs burned to the ground and the Canadian government decided that subsequent development would take place under public control, although it did not build the present structure until the 1930s. Meanwhile, Dr Brett's sanitorium burned in 1933 and now is the site of the Cascade Gardens.

The Upper Hot Springs, recently renovated, draw thousands of visitors wanting to de-stress themselves. The outdoor pool, with its reasonable entry fee, is particularly popular. Those with a bit more money to spend will enjoy the spa facilities with offerings ranging from aromatherapy to mineral water plunges. The pool's hot water can be enjoyed in winter as well as summer even though the surrounding air temperature can be more than a little nippy. Interpretive exhibits explain the history of the springs. Facilities for disabled travellers along with a cafe, patio, and shops fill out the services available at this venerable attraction. If you would like to explore undeveloped hot springs, then the Middle Hot Springs above the Banff town site, not far from the Upper Springs, are a good place to go. They can be reached via a three-kilometre walk from the Cascade Gardens up Sulphur Mountain. Once here, you will find a cave and the typical tufa rock found in a natural setting along with some majestic views to reward you for your climb up the mountain.

Upper Hot Springs and Pool, a good place to sooth your aching limbs after a vigorous mountain hike.

The shallow Vermilion Lakes, near the Banff town site.

Following four pages: the Vermilion Lakes with Mount Rundle in the background, as enjoyed through the light and shadow of an evolving day.

VERMILION LAKES AND MOUNT RUNDLE

The Vermilion Lakes, an extensive region of montane wetlands, lie west of the Banff town site. Their name comes from ochre beds at the iron-rich mineral springs at the Vermilion River pass where the Blackfoot and Kootenay tribes obtained materials for some of their ceremonial body paints. At one point in the past, the national parks staff used dams to keep the lake levels high enough to support boating and fishing. More recently, they removed the dams to reduce the degree of human intervention in the environment. The lakes subsequently dropped so that they now are quite shallow and the surrounding region has begun to fill in with aquatic vegetation.

This development is the normal first step in the evolution from a montane wetland to a floodplain forest, a process that should be completed within the next few hundred years. Nearby is the Fenland Trail, a two-kilometre path through floodplain forest which presents you with an opportunity to see what the Vermilion Lakes will look like in the future. This trail is just one of 80 at Banff which traverse 1300 kilometres of the park to take you off through all kinds of fascinating ecological zones.

At 2949 metres, Mount Rundle stands proudly behind the Vermilion Lakes. It got its name in 1859 to honour Robert Rundle, an English Methodist missionary who worked among the plains tribes in the 1840s. Located between Canmore and the Banff townsite, it probably is the most famous mountain in Banff. It and another celebrated local peak, Castle Mountain, are good examples of the two dominant mountain forms in the park. Mount Rundle presents the typical configuration of the front ranges of the Rockies, with its slanting table-top shape. Castle Mountain is characteristic of the castellated main ranges with its layer-cake profile.

The Canadian Rockies start at the southern end of British Columbia and Alberta and extend north 1200 kilometres to the Liard River Basin near the Yukon Territory. At the centre of the Rockies is the Continental (or Great) Divide. Here, the height of land separates Canada into two primary parts: a westerly portion which drains rivers into the Pacific Ocean; and an easterly division which sends water to the Arctic and Atlantic oceans.

The divide also acts as much of the border between BC and Alberta. The cattle country of Alberta's rolling foothills lies east of the Rockies about 1000 to 1500 metres below the mountains. The foothills eventually join the vast grain-growing regions of the Canadian prairies at an average distance of 50 kilometres from the Rocky Mountains.

LAKE MINNEWANKA

Lake Minnewanka, a bit northeast of downtown Banff, is the largest body of water in the park. Its name comes from the Cree expression for 'lake of the water spirit.' Today, it is larger than it was in historical times because the outlet of the original lake was dammed in 1912, and in 1941 the lake was enlarged further. A good way to see the lake and surrounding region is along the Lake Minnewanka Loop, a 25-kilo-metre drive past Cascade Mountain and other interesting sites.

There are several recreational opportunities at the lake to amuse you today. Fishing is popular, particularly as this lake is the only one in Banff where power boats are allowed. There is also a 90-minute boat tour you can take to view the sights and wildlife. If scuba diving is your thing, you can visit the site of a former resort, Minnewanka Landing, that now lies submerged below the waters as a result of the lake's 20th-century expansions. (The lake is 25 metres higher than it was before damming.)

Looking across Lake Minnewanka you can see the Palliser Range of Mountains, named after Captain John Palliser. Back in 1857, this Irish-born explorer led a three-year scientific expedition to the Canadian west on behalf of the British government. His objectives were to determine if this poorly understood region could be settled and whether or not roads and railways could be cut through the Rockies to link the British territories in North America from the Atlantic to the Pacific. The result of his journey was the first large scale scientific report on the Canadian west. One of its conclusions was that the immense interior east of the Rockies could sustain an agricultural population. That news subsequently helped both the British and Canadian governments plan to end Hudson's Bay Company control over the region and open it up to settlement.

Between the Banff townsite and Lake Minnewanka is the site of the former town of Bankhead, a coal mining community that existed between 1903 and 1922. Here, you can imagine what life was like back then by following an interpretive trail that passes through the site. The buildings are mostly gone now, but in its glory days it boasted 40 homes, two large boarding houses, a church, a school, and sporting facilities to cater to the 600 people who lived and worked in Bankhead. The population at the time consisted largely of immigrant workers from Germany, Poland, Italy, and China. When the town closed, the buildings were sold off and moved. Some survive today in the Banff town site.

In and around pretty Lake Minnewanka.

This and following three pages: Johnston Canyon, a great place to explore en route from Banff to Lake Louise.

JOHNSTON CANYON

There are two ways to travel north from the Banff town site to Lake Louise: the Trans-Canada Highway and the Bow Valley Parkway. The latter is the more relaxed and scenic route and will take you past such popular attractions as Johnston Canyon and Castle Mountain. En route, you will pass through hilly terrain known as the Hillsdale Slide. About 8000 years ago, a large part of a mountain collapsed to form the hills you see today. This happened after the mountain had been undermined thousands of years earlier during the last ice age. Geologists have documented the site as one of the Rockies' largest landslides.

Johnston Canyon, about 25 kilometres north of the Banff town site, is well worth a stop along the parkway. This land form, roughly 30 metres deep, and as narrow as six metres wide in places, is accessible along a good walkway that takes you past seven waterfalls, including the 30-metre upper falls, and allows you to explore how water erodes rock over many centuries. Along the way you can see a grouping of six springs, the Inkpots, coloured a deep aqua by glacial sediments. The hike to the Inkpots can take four hours; so if you don't have the time, you might limit your walking to a trip to the lower falls at 1.5 kilometres from the parkway. The route takes you across a number of catwalks which jut right out into the gorge where you will be splashed by the spray from the cataracts. One of the attractions at the canyon, as in the Rockies as a whole, is the profusion of pretty wildflowers you will encounter. Like many trails in the national parks system, you'll find interpretive plaques along the way to make your visit more enjoyable by explaining details about the environment to you.

Many tourists to Canada come with strange notions about it always being cold here. Summer in much of Canada can be downright hot with 30 degrees Celsius, or more, being fairly common depending on where you visit.

Because of the elevation of the Rockies, however, things are a bit unusual here. One summer day might hit 30 degrees; but then, it might snow the next. And, because the mountains sometimes create their own micro environments, it might be bright and sunny where you are but pour rain a kilometre away. Spring here tends to come late; autumn can be glorious with bright cool days.

Winter comes early in the Rockies, with average daytime temperatures in January hovering around minus 15 but with some cold snaps dropping the mercury to minus 35 or 40. Wind chill makes it seem colder. In any case, the weather changes rapidly and frequently, so be prepared.

Castle Mountain on the Bow River was known as Eisenhower Mountain between 1946 and 1979.

CASTLE MOUNTAIN

On the way to Lake Louise from Banff you will pass Castle Mountain - a glorious hunk of limestone, dolomite, and shale which, as its name suggests, looms over the Bow River like a mediaeval fortress. Popular with climbers, Castle Mountain rises to a height of 2766 metres above sea level.

The name 'Castle Mountain' dates to 1858 and is the title in use today. However, between 1946 and 1979, it had a different appellation: Eisenhower Mountain. The change came on orders from Prime Minister William Lyon Mackenzie King who wanted to honour Dwight D. Eisenhower, the supreme allied commander on the western front in World War II, when he visited Canada just after the return of peace. However, this caused considerable resentment because it replaced a long-standing and popular title and because people felt uncomfortable naming a mountain after a living person. Today Eisenhower's name is associated only with the separate 2752-metre tower at the east side of the main massif.

If you are an experienced rock climber, then you can scale the mountain. If you're not, there is a moderate 7.2-kilometre hike up to the base of the sheer walls for a splendid view of the surrounding countryside.

This trail departs from the Bow Valley Parkway, about five kilometres above Castle Mountain Junction on the road to Lake Louise.

In the past, Canadians were described romantically as 'hewers of wood and drawers of water' because so much of the economy was based on natural resources. Despite the country's 20th-century diversification into manufacturing, service industries, and other endeavours, primary resources continue to form the cornerstone of the nation's prosperity. Although extractive industries largely have disappeared from the national parks in the Rockies, traces of their former operations survive. Here, near Castle Mountain, there once was a boom town called Silver City. It was founded in 1883 to serve the needs of the CPR when the railway reached this spot. Shortly after, rumours of silver in the area precipitated an influx of prospectors so that the population quickly reached 2000. Within two years, the railway had moved on, the promise of silver had proved to be false, and Silver City lay deserted. Deserted, that is, except for one old coot, Joe Wilson, who hunted and trapped in the area until the 1930s. The Silver City site is in a meadow near the Bow River Parkway.

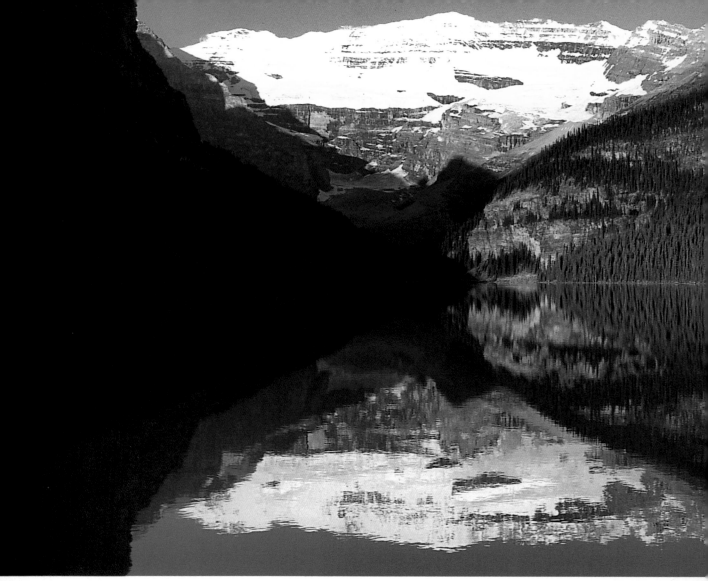

Lake Louise in its summer brilliance.

LAKE LOUISE AND VICTORIA GLACIER

About 55 kilometres northwest of the town of Banff is one of Canada's most famous natural attractions: Lake Louise. The deep green lake, surrounded by mountains and glaciers, has drawn sightseers for over a century who have marvelled at the natural beauty and have wondered why the lake is such a strong, almost shocking green colour. It comes from sunlight hitting the lake's floating mineral deposits of 'rock flour' which come suspended in the meltwaters from Victoria Glacier.

Lake Louise is the daughter of Victoria Glacier. In the distant past, the glacier covered the whole lake. It gradually deposited debris to form a landscape feature called a 'terminal moraine' which acted as a dam

to hold meltwater as the glacier slowly retreated. Today the lake, created by the moraine and sitting at an elevation of 1731 metres, is 2.4 kilometres long, 500 metres wide, and 90 metres deep. Native peoples called it 'the Lake of Little Fishes.' Its modern name honours Princess Louise Caroline Alberta, a daughter of Queen Victoria who married the Marquis of Lorne. The marquis served as Canada's governor-general from 1878 to 1883 during that great age of westward expansion when the lake became prominent after the Canadian Pacific Railway reached it in 1883.

In 1890, a wood chalet opened to serve the needs of Victorian tourists. The building burned in 1893, but was succeeded by a new guest house which could accom-

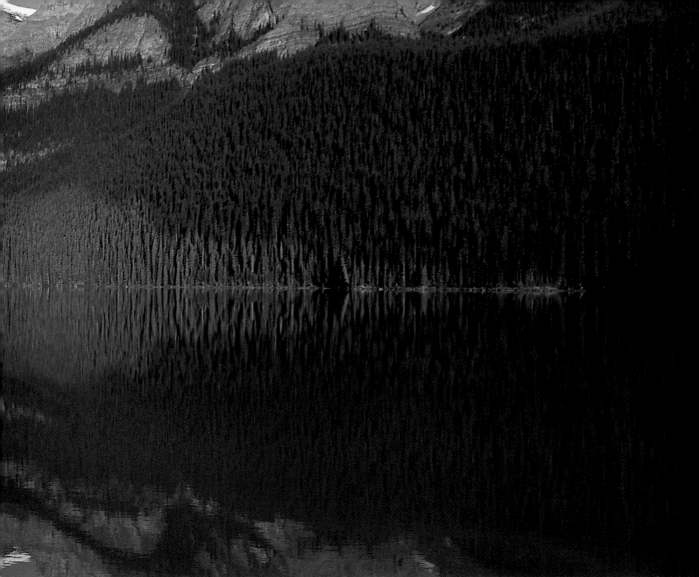

Under Victoria Glacier at the water's edge.

Following pages: the Lake Louise panorama with the Chateau Lake Louise in the foreground, as seen from the local gondola ride.

modate 12 travellers. Gradually, the CPR replaced, then enlarged the guest house so that by 1913 the Tu-doresque Chateau Lake Louise could sleep 400 tourists. Rising more than 3460 metres above sea level behind Lake Louise is Mount Victoria. First conquered in 1897, it became a favourite target for the 'alpiners' who came to the Rockies in quest of a successful climbing holiday. The people behind the conquest of 1897 brought along a Swiss mountaineer by the name of Peter Sarbach to help ensure success. Sarbach's work inspired the CPR to hire a number of Swiss guides in 1899 to help attract tourists to Lake Louise. These people became a fixture at the lake until mountain guiding died out in the 1950s.

A boathouse where you can rent a canoe. Below: peaceful explorations.

Lake Louise and Victoria Glacier, views to capture the imagination.

Beyond its visual and mountaineering pleasures, Lake Louise is the centre of Canada's largest ski area, kept in prime condition by an average winter's snowfall of 4.2 metres. Lake Louise is also a good starting point for hikers seeking out the remote high country along the Continental Divide. Even if you're not a hiker, you will enjoy a walk along the Lake Louise shore line. If you want more exercise, then set off on some of the 70 kilometres of marked hiking trails which offer countless breathtaking panoramas for your pleasure. One particularly popular hike is the Plain of Six Glaciers Trail to a stunning lookout over Victoria Glacier and Lake Louise. If you get hungry en route, there is a tearoom (open during the summer) about five kilometres from the chateau. If you don't want to walk or ski, you can hire a canoe, a boat, or a horse to survey Lake Louise and its environs for a few hours or a day. If you have the time, you can mount a horse for a guided trail ride, lasting anywhere from three days to two weeks. Another excursion is the Lake Louise Gondola Lift to take you up over 2000 metres to Mount Whitehorn where views stretch over Lake Louise and across to the Valley of the Ten Peaks and the Bow Valley.

Many people think Lake Louise is even more delightful in winter, and find pleasure skating on the lake's cold weather ice rink. This page: the artistry of ice sculptures and the thrill of downhill skiing.

Mount Victoria and its dramatic glacier.

CHATEAU LAKE LOUISE

Today's Chateau Lake Louise, capable of housing 1000 guests, is one of Canadian Pacific's most famous hotels and one of North America's best loved places to stay. Like its famous cousin, the Banff Springs Hotel, the chateau had its founding in the late 19th century as a destination for travellers who took the CPR west from Toronto, Montreal, and other population centres in central Canada as well as from the United States and abroad. Ever on the lookout to improve the tourist trade, the railway added such creature comforts to the hotel as electricity in 1916-17 and a narrow-gauge tram to move people from the old railway station to the hotel (and which ran between 1912 and 1930). The chateau is one spot where you will want to blow your budget and luxuriate in its warmth. However, as almost every other visitor to the Rockies with a bit of extra cash wants to do the same thing, you need to make reservations months in advance if you plan to stay during the summer or winter high seasons. Recently remodelled, the chateau offers year-round comforts, restaurants, a spa, shopping, and various forms of entertainment to keep you happy. Even if you don't spend the night at the hotel, you should visit to enjoy its charming gardens, savour its public rooms, and have tea, a meal, or indulge in another of the chateau's services.

Summer and winter in and about the popular Chateau Lake Louise.

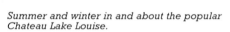

OLD RAIL STATION
AND POST HOTEL

The old log railway station at Lake Louise served travellers for about a century until train service to the village came to a halt in the 1980s. Now, this handsome historic building from a bygone era has become a bar and restaurant. Its old waiting room accommodates both pizza and fine dining, while the former ticketing lobby is the place to retreat for a quiet drink. Outside, on the track, are two vintage railway dining cars where you can relish excellent grilled meats.

Begun in 1942 as a humble ski lodge, the Post Hotel was completely remodelled by new European owners between 1988 and 1993 to become one of the more luxurious places to stay in the Rockies. Built in traditional log and beam construction, the hotel boasts charming public rooms, a renowned restaurant, a two-storey wood-panelled library, and gorgeous views of the peaks over Lake Louise and Moraine Lake.

Always known for superb dining, the revitalized Post Hotel has built on that tradition and now offers some of the finest food in the Rockies. A bit pricey, but worth the cost, this is the place to eat full-flavoured meats and fish such as salmon in a champagne and passion fruit sauce.

While you savour the comfort of the Post Hotel, you can reflect on how far we've come since the first tourist visited Lake Louise. He was A.P. Coleman, a geology professor from Toronto, who arrived in 1884. Professor Coleman paid 50 cents to share a bed with some smelly drunk in a log shack for the night! (The next day, he found another place to stay.)

The Old Rail Station and Post Hotel below Lake Louise.

Overlooking the Wenkchemna Valley.

WENKCHEMNA PEAKS (VALLEY OF THE 10 PEAKS)

Wenkchemna is the word for 'ten' in the language of the Stoney people. One of the largest mountains in the Rockies, Mount Temple, sits here, towering over the northwest edge of the Wenkchemna Valley. Its girth consumes 15 square kilometres of the Rockies topography, and, at 3350 metres, it is the third tallest mountain in Banff National Park.

The Wenkchemna Peaks are a good example of the scenic majesty that Victorian Canadians wanted to protect when they established national parks, starting with Banff in 1885. Originally, the federal government, Canadian Pacific Railway officials, and other interested people saw the need to set aside land that never could be acquired by private concerns (although the CPR seems to have played a particularly strong role in ensuring that development fulfilled its corporate interests).

Between 1885 and 1887, the government created six mountain reserves that form the nuclei of today's Banff, Yoho, Kootenay, Glacier, Mount Revelstoke, and Waterton Lakes national parks. To a large degree, these initiatives were possible back then because much of western Canada consisted of federally-owned undeveloped territory. By the early 20th century, the government began to establish parks elsewhere in the country, and gradually created national parks in most of Canada's distinct ecological regions. To protect the parks for all time, activities that might degrade these natural areas, such as mining, forestry, and hunting, either are forbidden or are controlled carefully. Mining licences, for example, have not been issued in the parks since 1930 and the last mining enterprise, at Yoho, ceased operations in 1952. Nevertheless, in some areas of heavy tourist traffic, such as Banff, there has been acrimonious debate in recent years between the advocates and opponents of development over how much growth or environmental compromise is acceptable.

Most visitors experience the national parks within or near the towns and roadways. Most of the parks' land mass, however, sits in the back country. There, you will encounter few tourists and have superb opportunities to trek along high river valleys, through alpine meadows, and march up close to frigid icefields. You can strike out on your own into the wilderness if you wish, but you need to obtain a permit from the park authorities first. At the same time you get your permit, you can pick up the necessary topographical maps, guides, and brochures. Be sure to read the pamphlet about what to do if you encounter a bear! (Climbing up a tree isn't a good idea; most bears climb better than us.)

Canoeing is a relaxing way to enjoy Moraine Lake near Lake Louise.

Following pages: the Wenkchemna Peaks behind Moraine Lake.

MORAINE LAKE

Less than 15 kilometres from Lake Louise is Moraine Lake in the Valley of the Wenkchemna Mountains. Many visitors, to their surprise, feel that it is even more exquisite and spectacular than its larger and more famous cousin. Therefore, be sure to make the trip! Here, you will marvel at the unforgettable sight of the glacial lake framed by the dramatic Wenkchemna Peaks soaring up towards the heavens.

The lake is misnamed! The person who christened it in 1899, Walter Wilcox, thought it, like Lake Louise, had its origins because of a terminal glacial moraine. (A moraine is a kind of dam created by the debris left behind by a glacier which blocks up a valley so that a lake can form behind it.) However, this lake formed after a rock fall from its neighbour, the 'Tower of Babel,' dammed the run-off from the surrounding mountains to create Moraine Lake. You can explore the story of the lake's formation along a short interpretive trail to the top of the tower's rock and debris hill. After hiking along this or one of the other local trails, you might want to retreat to the Moraine Lake Lodge on the lake shore to relax and enjoy a meal. Other nearby facilities include a good picnic area, interpretive exhibits, canoe rentals, and tourist accommodation.

CROWFOOT GLACIER

One of the leading attractions along the Icefields Parkway is the Crowfoot Glacier. It got its name because it resembled a huge three-toed claw - a crow's foot - when discovered a century or so ago. Today, the name seems a bit inappropriate because the glacier has retreated since the 1870s and one of the 'toes' broke off in the 1940s. Thus, it now resembles a two-pronged wishbone, but it nevertheless remains one of the most popular of the 100 or so glaciers along the parkway.

For years travel between Banff and Jasper was difficult, if not nearly impossible. Then, in the 1930s, construction began on the Banff-Jasper Highway as a make-work project during the Depression. The gravel road opened for automobile traffic in 1940. As tourism and traffic grew, this route, with its twists and turns, proved inadequate to meet changing demands. In the early 1960s, the new Icefields Parkway, placed largely on top of the old road, replaced the Banff-Jasper Highway and today is one of the most spellbinding routes motorists can take.

BOW LAKE

When the Icefields Parkway (also known as Highway 93) leaves Lake Louise, it proceeds north along the Bow River. At the headwaters of the river sits Bow Lake, one of the larger glacial lakes you will encounter along the road. It is fed by the Bow Glacier at the top of the valley which itself is connected to the Wapta Icefield farther west. At the lake, you can see the Bow Glacier which serves as one of five outlets for the 40-square-kilometre icefield.

Trout fishing is popular at the south end of the lake. Moose can be seen at the lake's swampier parts. Moose are the largest animals with antlers in the world, with adult male moose typically standing two metres tall at the shoulder. They like Bow Lake and the roadsides along the parkway, so chances are good that you will see one en route from Banff to Jasper. It looks like a great clumsy creature, but a moose can manage dense bush with ease, conquer deep snows, swim well, and, if it wants, run at speeds that exceed 50 kilometres per hour! Even though they are vegetarians, stay inside your car if you meet one; otherwise, you might meet your doom, especially if you disturb a female protecting its calf, or if you bother them during rutting season.

Two views of Crowfoot Glacier. Below: glacially-fed Bow Lake.

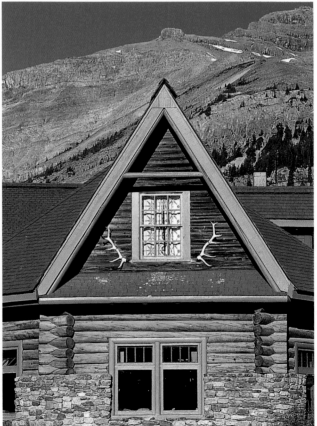

Num-ti-jah Lodge on Bow Lake. Num-ti-jah is an aboriginal word for the local marten, a member of the weasel family.

Following pages: Peyto Lake as seen from the Bow Summit Trail, 300 metres above the valley floor.

NUM-TI-JAH LODGE

Jimmy Simpson, an early outfitter and guide, built Num-ti-jah Lodge beside Bow Lake in 1920 when the region still was isolated wilderness. It replaced a more primitive camp that he and his wife, Billie, had operated on the spot for the previous two decades. Simpson arrived in the region in 1899 and became famous for his ability to find big game to satisfy the rich American hunters who holidayed at the camp. He died in 1972 at the age of 95; and in 1974 had a mountain named after him.

PEYTO LAKE

Before descending into the North Saskatchewan River drainage region along the Icefields Parkway, you will encounter Peyto Lake, celebrated for its natural beauty and turquoise water. The lake got its name from a famous guide and park warden, Ebenezer William (or 'Wild Bill') Peyto. He came to the Rockies in the 1890s and remained until his death in 1943. Like many of the early outfitters, this Englishman was renowned for his individualism as well as his fondness for fringed buckskins and the other clichés of western garb, complete with a six-shooter on his hip.

A view of Mount Chephren.
Opposite: upper: in the North Saskatchewan River Valley;
lower: a classic western building at the Crossing.

MOUNT CHEPHREN

Mount Chephren, at 3307 metres, lies behind Chephren Lake, west of the Waterfowl lakes beside the Icefields Parkway. Considered one of the finest mountains in the Rockies from an aesthetic perspective, it is visible for much of the parkway between Bow Pass and Big Bend Hill. Originally named Pyramid Mountain, its name was changed to Mount Chephren in 1918 to avoid confusion with another mountain with the same name in Jasper. Nevertheless, the new title kept alive the link to its earlier one because it is named after the son and successor of Cheops, the builder of Egypt's Great Pyramid.

You can get close to Mount and Lake Chephren along the Chephren Lake Trail which runs west from a point 1.2 kilometres south of the Waterfowl Lake Campground. The trail takes you four kilometres to Lake Chephren along swampy meadows and dense forest. At about the halfway point of the trail, if you have the energy, you can take another hike, this time along the Cirque Lake Trail which, at 10 kilometres, leads to a beautiful subalpine lake with superb fishing opportunities. These trails are just two of a large number of accessible hiking opportunities you will find along the Icefields Parkway.

SASKATCHEWAN RIVER CROSSING

In the old days, one of the more trying challenges facing people in the Rockies was the North Saskatchewan River, a difficult waterway to cross, particularly at high water. The result: many small and large tragedies occurred as people and horses attempted to pass through it. ('Saskatchewan' comes from the Cree language, and means 'swift current.') Even in the 1930s, bridging the river for the Banff-Jasper Highway proved to be an unusually demanding and exhausting project. Today, as motorists whiz across the bridge, it is almost impossible to imagine how different things were back then. Although the river itself proved to be a problem, the climate in the area is warmer and drier than elsewhere in the Rockies. With its higher temperatures and lighter snowfalls, this region is a magnet for deer, bighorn sheep, and mountain goats which also, of course, makes it an excellent place for nature lovers who want to see these wild creatures.

The 285-kilometre Icefields Parkway does not have many facilities for tourists, although there are a number of simple hotels for hikers and cyclists. (Cyclists usually take two or three days to travel the parkway.) However, the Saskatchewan River Crossing, about 153 kilometres south of Jasper, offers travellers accommodation, food, gas, souvenirs, and other services.

MISTAYA CANYON

If you are in a hurry, you can drive the Icefields Parkway in three or four hours. But if you do, you will miss all the great things to see along the way, such as the Mistaya Canyon. Situated a few kilometres south of the Saskatchewan River Crossing, it is one of the prettiest canyons in the west. It was created over many centuries because the Mistaya River carved its way through the local limestone to form the valley. The river, like so many in the region, starts off in a glacier above Peyto Lake. The word, 'Mistaya' by the way, is a Stoney expression for 'much wind.'

At the canyon, you can enjoy a 1.5-kilometre trail, easy enough for a family to traverse in an hour. The footpath starts off on an old road. Here, you will pass through a subalpine forest to the very narrow canyon. At the canyon, you can admire the sight of the Mistaya River as it plunges over the canyon walls on its way to the North Saskatchewan River. The latter river is 1216 kilometres long. Over 80 percent of its volume comes from the Rockies as meltwater.

The dramatic Mistaya Canyon near the Icefields Parkway.

INDEX